The DOCTORS

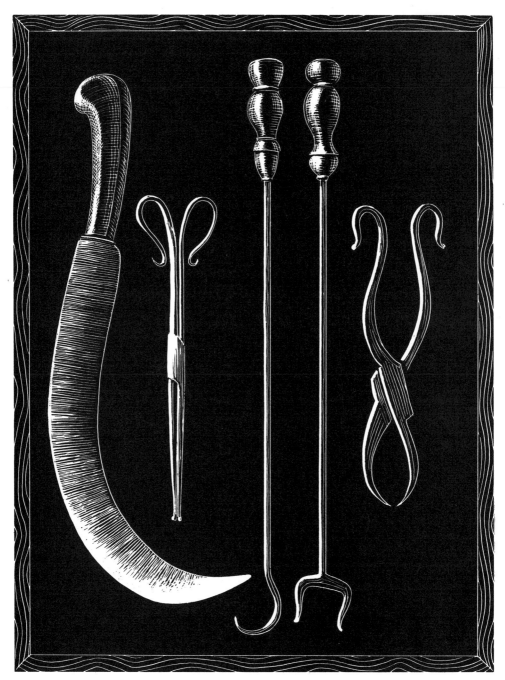

Some eighteenth-century surgical instruments.

COLONIAL CRAFTSMEN

The
DOCTORS

WRITTEN & ILLUSTRATED BY

Leonard Everett Fisher

BENCHMARK BOOKS

MARSHALL CAVENDISH
NEW YORK

Benchmark Books
Marshall Cavendish Corporation
99 White Plains Road
Tarrytown, New York 10591-9001

─────────

Library of Congress Cataloging-in-Publication Data
Fisher, Leonard Everett.
The doctors / written and illustrated by Leonard Everett Fisher.
p.   cm. — (Colonial craftsmen)
Originally published: New York : Franklin Watts, 1966
Includes index.
Summary: Traces the early development of medicine in colonial America and
discusses some of the methods and medications used at that time for treating illness.
ISBN 0-7614-0481-3 (lib. bdg.)
1. Medicine—United States—History—Juvenile literature. 2. Physicians—United
States—History—Juvenile literature. [1. Medicine—History. 2. Physicians.]
I. Title. II. Series: Fisher, Leonard Everett. Colonial craftsmen.
R152.F56 1997 610'.973—dc20 96-13081 CIP AC

─────────

Printed and bound in the United States of America

1   3   5   6   4   2

Other titles in this series

*Many voyagers suffered
from shipboard illnesses.*

To most European people, North America in the seventeenth century was a forbidding continent — a vast wilderness that seemed to offer only dangers and hardships. But there were some people who looked hopefully toward America. It promised a new way of living that might be more rewarding than life in Europe. They were willing to risk its dangers.

For the most part, only energetic, adventuresome, and healthy persons undertook the long journey to America. Those who survived the hard ocean voyage without illness or injury were considered lucky. Many came down with scurvy or other shipboard diseases and injuries. And most of these people were never certain of regaining their good health after arriving in the New World. There were few doctors to help them.

From time to time during the early years of the first English colony, at Jamestown, "physitians" (physicians) and "chirurgeons" (surgeons), skilled in the practice of "physick" and "chirurgery" (medicine and surgery), arrived.

Among these men were Dr. Thomas Wotton, who served as surgeon to the tiny fleet of three ships that brought the first settlers to the shores of Virginia in 1607, and Dr. Anthony Bagnall, who became surgeon of the Jamestown fort. Neither of these men remained in the colony for long. In fact, when Captain John Smith was injured by a gunpowder explosion in 1609 he returned to England for treatment. There was no doctor in the colony at that time.

The need for a doctor was keenly felt by the Jamestown adventurers. The colonists were plagued without letup by injuries, starvation, infections, and the diseases that followed them. Death was a constant companion. In 1620, the London Company, sponsor of the Jamestown colony, appointed Dr. Lawrence Bohune as physician-general of Virginia. For the next few years, Dr. Bohune stayed in the colony and did all he could to help the desperate settlers.

But his work was not easy. For one thing, the Jamestown colonists had difficulty in enduring the constantly changing climate and the wilderness conditions of the new land, and Jamestown

itself had been settled in a damp and unhealthful spot. For another thing, Dr. Bohune relied on the ancient medical ideas that were still held by nearly every doctor of the early seventeenth century. These ideas were thoroughly unscientific and did not really offer help in curing a patient.

According to one of these notions, disease was caused by too much of one of the humors, or fluids, that were contained in the body. And the best way to get rid of the fluid was thought to be by bleeding the patient — removing some of his blood. In reality, this did nothing but weaken him further.

In many instances, the patient was given a food that resembled the part of his body that was troublesome. If he had a headache, he was given the meat of a walnut, because a walnut meat looked somewhat like a miniature brain. Or if he had a bothersome kidney, he might be given kidney beans, shaped somewhat like kidneys, to cure his trouble. These "natural" would-be cures, which rarely worked, were based on a medical idea that was at least one thousand years old.

According to this idea, if a disease occurred in any region of the world, a natural remedy for the disease could be found in the same region. The remedy could be detected by its appearance — its resemblance to the afflicted part of the body.

Sometimes a sick person was given a violent rubdown. At other times, the poor unfortunate was put in either a scalding-hot or an icy-cold bath. For rheumatism, a hot poultice was applied, to blister the skin. Although this did not really help the patient, at least it gave him a different pain to think about.

In fact, in all the English American colonies during the early seventeenth century, the doctors' remedies were often so painful or so drastic that they were almost worse than the illnesses themselves. Many persons preferred to let nature take its course rather than risk a doctor's cures. Ill persons recovered with whatever nursing their friends or families could give them, unless the trouble was serious. Then they might die. If a man suffered a wound, there was always the chance of infection. As a result, he might lose the use of an arm or a leg, or again, he might die.

Walnut

Not much was known about the human body or its ailments and their causes and cures.

Most of the medicinal remedies of the day were made from herbs and the roots of plants. Often the remedies sent from England were in short supply at Jamestown. Because of this and because the London Company was interested in any medicines that might be found in the New World, the settlers began searching for native plants that might be helpful.

By now, the newcomers had grown to know the Indians of the region. And both the doctors and the other settlers had begun to realize that the Indians often knew more than the Englishmen did about which local remedies were helpful for various illnesses. Indian medicine men, or *shamans*, used a variety of treatments for wounds and for ailments that included everything from arthritis and rheumatism to snakebite and broken bones. The shamans relied partly on prayers and dancing, but to cure many illnesses they depended on powerful drugs and potions. They made these remedies from leaves and roots, herbs, tree bark, and parts of some animals — all found in the wil-

derness round about. The leaves and juice of to-
bacco were widely used for treating ailments, and
so were the petals of certain flowers. Sweathouses
and hot mud were used in the treatment of many
an Indian malady. Some of the shamans' remedies worked so well that the doctors and the sick
and miserable colonists of early Virginia were
glad to adopt them.

As the years passed, a number of men calling
themselves physicians arrived in Virginia. Although they were badly needed, these Englishmen came chiefly to make a fortune from the
land rather than to aid the settlers. From time
to time, they treated the people stricken in the
awful epidemics that swept through the settlements, and they cared for the men who had been
maimed or wounded as a result of Indian attacks.
In many cases, however, the doctors demanded
too high a fee for their uncertain skills, and they
refused to treat those who could not afford to
pay. At times, they did not bother at all with the
sick and injured. Few colonists could count on
quick medical attention by the doctors who had
settled among them. Land, treasure, politics, and

power seemed to interest most of these men more.

In 1639, and up until 1662, the Virginia assembly passed a series of laws to make their doctors practice medicine with more responsibility. These laws made doctors liable to arrest if they "were more swayed by politick than Christian charity," and they compelled doctors to "declare on oath the value of their medicine." The laws were necessary to protect the colonists from some of the more greedy and less skillful doctors. But in 1660 the Virginia assembly also passed a law to protect the doctors from the people. This law allowed a doctor to collect his fee even though the patient might have died. Much later, in the 1730's, the government of Virginia passed a law that regulated all medical fees.

Those colonists who lived in lonely places distant from the settlements, or who lived on the large farms and plantations of the South, often never saw a doctor throughout their lives. In treating illnesses, these colonists put their faith in their own skills and knowledge. For the most part, they used tree barks, plant leaves, roots, and herbs as medicines. Books called herbals,

which listed plant remedies, were found in many homes. Sometimes the hot teas, juices, powders, and pastes the settlers made from plants seemed to work; sometimes they did not. Perhaps something else might. Through their own experimenting, the settlers learned at least a few tried-and-true remedies for some ailments.

Farther to the north, along the raw and windy shore of New England, other settlers were waging a similar battle for survival.

In December, 1620, the Pilgrim Separatists, one hundred and three in number, stumbled from their ocean voyage onto an icy beach at Plymouth, in what is now Massachusetts. They were sick and weary from their long journey in a rolling, lurching tub of a merchantman called the *Mayflower*. Fifty-two of their number died before spring.

Among the survivors of that first deadly winter at Plymouth was Samuel Fuller, deacon of the church, and physician to the colony. He had taken some medical training in England and on the Continent. In 1621, Dr. Fuller, then forty-one years old, tirelessly fought two dreadful diseases

— smallpox and typhoid fever — that threatened to wipe out the settlement at Plymouth. During the next twelve years, he traveled from one Massachusetts settlement to another. He bled the sick — colonists and Indians alike — and tried to keep the people alive with a mixture of prayer and doses of medicine. In 1633, Fuller himself died during a smallpox epidemic.

After Fuller's death, the settlers of the Massachusetts Bay region were not left entirely without a doctor. Shortly after the founding of Boston in 1630, several English physicians appeared in the colony. Among them was eighteen-year-old Giles Firmin, who had studied medicine in England. Firmin not only cared for the sick and injured, but also held classes in human anatomy, the structure of the human body.

Later, a number of the young men who had listened to Firmin's anatomy lectures studied at Harvard College, newly founded in Cambridge, Massachusetts. Upon graduating, they became ministers of the Puritan church. In addition, they acted as schoolmasters or, using their earlier anatomy lessons, they treated the sick. Through-

A medical apprentice
made up the doctor's medicines.

out most of the colonies, many of the clergymen also worked as doctors in the early days of settlement. Some of them had studied at least some medicine before leaving England or the Continent.

But too many people were dying. Physicians who were more highly trained were badly needed. There were no medical schools in the colonies during those early years. To get an education in medicine, a person usually became a medical apprentice, much as other persons became apprentices in crafts such as shoemaking, wigmaking, or printing. A medical apprentice lived in a doctor's house, did odd jobs for the doctor, and often acted as his servant. In addition, the apprentice learned how to make up the doctor's medicines; he read the doctor's few medical books and observed the doctor as he treated his patients.

After he had gained enough knowledge, the former apprentice went out to practice as a doctor himself. Some of the doctors who had been trained through an apprenticeship were skillful; others were not. All of them became doctors

Many doctors became interested in
plants and their medicinal uses.

merely by proclaiming themselves as such. Any
other persons who cared to could do the same
thing. There was no group of persons whose duty
it was to judge a doctor's abilities before he began his practice, and to turn away those persons
who were incompetent.

If it was not possible to work as an apprentice,
some persons interested in becoming doctors
simply read a few of the medical books available
at the time, and learned how to make medicines
for various illnesses. Some young colonial ministers were sent back to England to study for
medical degrees. There they learned the latest
methods of prevention and cure of disease — all
of them methods that were still based on ancient
ideas. They also learned the newest ideas about
how the body functioned.

Even more important, perhaps, was the ac-
quaintance these medical students made with
European doctors who were becoming more and
more interested in botany, the science and study
of plant life. At this time, seamen and explorers
were returning to Europe with unknown herbs,
flowers, shrubs, and trees from many parts of the

world. The doctors were interested in the possible use of these plants as medicines.

Unfortunately, only a few of the colonial medical students returned to America after they had completed their education abroad. Many of them remained in England as botanists. Those who did return to America often spent more time on church affairs and on government than on medical practice. Because church and government were very close together in the seventeenth century, many of the minister-doctors were also busy with affairs of state.

Since the doctors seemed to be occupied with other things, many of the colonists looked elsewhere for help. Much of this help came from local craftsmen such as tailors and wigmaking barbers, who were licensed surgeons and who were also allowed to bleed patients.

In Europe, at this time, surgery was considered a dirty job, better suited to a skilled craftsman, to a rough-and-ready peddler of knives, or to a barber, than to a doctor. The seventeenth-century surgeon was considered inferior because he used his hands, while the physician used his head. In

America, there was not quite as sharp a line between the two fields of work. Often a doctor did whatever was necessary, without considering his dignified position.

A medical degree in very early America was no proof that its holder had much practical medical knowledge, anyway. A licensed craftsman-surgeon might possibly have more useful experience and skill in treating certain kinds of illnesses than most physicians had at that time.

The most popular doctor in early New England was not a physician at all, but a lawyer. He was John Winthrop II, son of the governor of Massachusetts Bay Colony, who had himself acted as a doctor to the colonists. Among the younger Winthrop's papers was an eight-page letter sent to his father in Massachusetts by Edward Stafford, a London doctor. In the letter, Dr. Stafford had listed dozens of recipes said to be cures for various disorders.

One of the recipes gave directions for making a black powder from toads. This was to be used "against the plague, small pox, purples, all sorts of feavers; poyson; either by way of prevention,

John Winthrop II
(1606–1676)

or after infection. . . ."

But, like most of the doctors of his time, Stafford relied chiefly on herbs and plants as medicines. Saint-John's-wort, an herb, was boiled in water until the brew became reddish in color. It was then given to persons thought to be mad, in the belief that it would cure their insanity. Those patients suffering from yellow jaundice were treated with an unpleasant preparation made from a quart of boiled milk mixed with salt and yellow saffron, a powder made from a plant. A powder made from "ye great Bryonie roote" was mixed with water and given to persons who suffered from dizziness. "Ye 4 great cold seeds" (watermelon, gourd, melon, and cucumber), together with barley and almond nuts, were made into a thick liquid to be swallowed by those whose bladders were thought to be diseased. A great number of herbs were used for various other ailments.

The younger Winthrop's popularity as a doctor may have rested chiefly on his reputation as a scholar and as the son of the governor, and on the fact that he did not charge patients for his

In serious epidemics, the belongings
of the ill were burned by workers
wearing protective shrouds.

services. In 1659, he became governor of the Connecticut colony and served in this office until his death in 1676. And he continued to give free medical advice, often by letter, to the countless numbers of people who asked for it. He prescribed syrup of violets, spirits of anise, powdered coral, wormwood, rhubarb, calomel, and horseradish, among other things.

But no matter how diligently some doctors tried to help the ailing, life for the average colonist was hard, and often it was short. Wave after wave of horrible epidemics swept through the colonies time and time again, killing many people. New England suffered the most, because it was the most densely settled. Here, thousands were stricken with malaria, yellow fever, diphtheria, influenza, smallpox, measles, and dysentery.

Over the years, the authorities passed a series of quarantine laws to help prevent the spread of contagious diseases. But try as they might, people could do little to stop the epidemics, once they had started. To many, the future of the settlements in the New World looked bleak in-

deed unless something was done.

A few persons experimented with ways of preventing the fatal diseases. Certainly the old ideas were not working, and the Almighty did not seem to pay much attention to the prayers of the colonists. In 1678, a Boston clergyman, Thomas Thacher, had a poster, or broadside, printed. It told the people what to do if they caught smallpox or measles. It was quite sensible in its ideas on fresh air and diet. Yet not until almost fifty years later, in 1721, did doctors make any real progress in controlling and preventing smallpox.

In that year, Zabdiel Boylston of Boston successfully inoculated his own son and several of his servants against the disease. In doing this, he was encouraged by Cotton Mather, a learned Puritan clergyman. Although inoculation had previously been used with some success in England, both Boylston and Mather were attacked because of their medical activities. One indignant citizen threw a bomb at Cotton Mather. He was unhurt, and Boylston continued to inoculate. He undoubtedly saved many lives and helped to convince people eventually that smallpox epidemics

could be controlled. Boylston had never gone to medical school, but had been taught medicine by his father.

From about 1721 on, doctors in eighteenth-century America changed greatly. While most of them still believed in the ancient medical ideas, some were inspired to new thinking by the scientific awakening that was taking place in Europe. The search for medicinal plants — especially herbs — was becoming more widespread, too, while the entire study of botany was growing more exact under the influence of medically trained scientists. Boylston's smallpox inoculations in 1721 had held out the promise of a life possibly free of some other diseases also. Many colonial citizens did all they could to make their hopes of better medical service come true.

Hospitals were established, and medical societies were founded. A little later, some of America's young colleges began to give medical instruction and to grant medical degrees. Through the study of anatomy, medical students learned more about how the human body worked. Here was at least a small beginning toward training

doctors for America.

In the meantime, the flame of political rebellion was burning bright throughout the colonies. By 1770, America was seething with anger over British mismanagement. Revolution was but a few short years away.

On July 4, 1776, the Americans declared themselves free of Great Britain and spent the next six years stubbornly fighting the British. From the very beginnings of that struggle, many politically minded American doctors served the cause of American independence.

Four colonial physicians signed the Declaration of Independence. They were Benjamin Rush of Pennsylvania; Lyman Hall of Georgia; and Matthew Thornton and Josiah Bartlett of New Hampshire. Oliver Wolcott of Connecticut, a lawyer who signed, had once been a medical student.

Almost immediately thereafter, a military medical department was established to care for the Revolutionary soldiers. Great numbers of doctors joined the Continental Army. Some served as fighting officers of the line, command-

Benjamin Rush
(1745–1813)

ing various regiments. Others looked after the sick, the wounded, and the hospitalized.

Dr. Benjamin Church of Boston was appointed the first medical director of the Continental Army, but he was soon court-martialed for treason. Dr. William Shippen, Jr., replaced him as chief of the medical department of the army. In 1777, Dr. Benjamin Rush of Philadelphia was appointed surgeon general of the Continental Army. He was thirty-three years old at the time.

The Revolutionary surgeon-doctors worked endlessly on the battlefields and in the hospitals to cure the ill and disabled and to save the lives of many of the sick and wounded. These medical men helped to keep the ragtag army together and on the march. Their battle was often against filth and primitive hospitals and lack of medical supplies rather than against the British enemy. The doctors did the best they could with what they had. For many of them, army service, though difficult, was a valuable experience. When the Revolutionary War was over, they returned home with better skills and a new compassion for their suffering patients. Although their in-

terest in the sick was often greater than their ability and their knowledge of how to prevent and cure illnesses, they never stopped trying to learn new ways.

Dr. Benjamin Rush, the army's surgeon general, went on to become one of the great teaching doctors of his time. Although he still believed in most of the old methods, he kept an open mind about new medical and scientific events. He cared so much for the well-being of the people that he did not oppose promising medical experiments or stand in the way of doctors whose ideas were different from his own. Some of his own ideas, too, were new, and proved eventually to be correct. An amazing man — patriot, physician, politician, teacher, chemist, fighter against slavery — he was an inspiration to the several thousand medical students who attended his lectures over a period of some forty years. He encouraged these younger men to improve medical science and the practice of medicine in America. Many of his former students always remembered his enthusiasm and were fired by it. Constantly they tried to become better doctors.

Some Colonial American Physicians and Surgeons

Bard, John (1716–1799)	*New York*
Bartlett, Josiah (1729–1795)	*New Hampshire*
Bond, Thomas (1712–1784)	*Pennsylvania*
Boylston, Zabdiel (1679–1766)	*Massachusetts*
Cadwalader, Thomas (1708?–1779)	*Pennsylvania*
Church, Benjamin (1734–?1778)	*Massachusetts*
Clayton, Joshua (1744–1798)	*Delaware*
Craik, James (1730–1814)	*Virginia*
Fernald, Reginald (1595–1656)	*New Hampshire*
Firmin, Giles (1615–1697)	*Massachusetts*
Fuller, Samuel (1580–1633)	*Massachusetts*
Garden, Alexander (1730?–1791)	*South Carolina*
Gardiner, Silvester (1708–1786)	*Massachusetts*
Hall, Lyman (1724–1790)	*Georgia*
Hopkins, Lemuel (1750–1801)	*Connecticut*
Lining, John (1708–1760)	*South Carolina*
Morgan, John (1735–1789)	*Pennsylvania*
Redman, John (1722–1808)	*Pennsylvania*
Rush, Benjamin (1745?–1813)	*Pennsylvania*
Scudder, Nathaniel (1733–1781)	*New Jersey*
Shippen, William, Jr. (1736–1808)	*Pennsylvania*
Tennent, John (1700?–?1760)	*Virginia*
Thacher, Thomas (1620–1678)	*Massachusetts*
Thornton, Matthew (1714?–1803)	*New Hampshire*
Warren, Joseph (1741–1775)	*Massachusetts*

INDEX

LEONARD EVERETT FISHER is a well-known author-artist whose books include *Alphabet Art, The Great Wall of China, The Tower of London, Marie Curie, Jason and the Golden Fleece, The Olympians, The ABC Exhibit, Sailboat Lost,* and many others.

Often honored for his contribution to children's literature, Mr. Fisher was the recipient of the 1989 Nonfiction Award presented by the *Washington Post* and the Children's Book Guild of Washington for the body of an author's work. In 1991, he received both the Catholic Library Association's Regina Medal and the University of Minnesota's Kerlan Award for the entire body of his work. Leonard Everett Fisher lives in Westport, Connecticut.